Transformations in Nature

An Egg Becomes a Robin

Amy Hayes

Cavendish Square

New York

Published in 2016 by Cavendish Square Publishing, LLC
243 5th Avenue, Suite 136, New York, NY 10016

Cataloging-in-Publication Data

Hayes, Amy.
An egg becomes a robin / by Amy Hayes.
p. cm. — (Transformations in nature)
Includes index.
ISBN 978-1-5026-0812-3 (hardcover) ISBN 978-1-5026-0810-9 (paperback) ISBN 978-1-5026-0813-0 (ebook)
1. Robins — Life cycles — Juvenile literature. 2. Robins — Juvenile literature. I. Hayes, Amy. II. Title.
QL696.P288 H39 2016
598.8'42—d23

Editorial Director: David McNamara
Copy Editor: Rebecca Rohan
Art Director: Jeffrey Talbot
Designer: Stephanie Flecha
Senior Production Manager: Jennifer Ryder-Talbot
Production Editor: Renni Johnson
Photo Research: J8 Media

Printed in the United States of America

Contents

Robins **hatch** from eggs.

5

A mother robin lays eggs in a **nest**.

7

The baby birds break
out of their eggs.

The mother robin
feeds the babies.

The baby birds
grow **feathers**.

13

They grow larger.

The nest gets **crowded**.

15

The baby birds
start learning to fly.

16

This young robin
has left the nest.

19

Now the robin
is all grown up.

21

New Words

crowded (CROWD-ed) To fill a place so that there is very little space.

feathers (FE-therz) Light growths that cover the bodies of birds.

hatch (HATCH) Break out of an egg.

nest (NEST) A home for birds made out of sticks and twigs.

Index

About the Author

Amy Hayes lives in the beautiful city of Buffalo, New York. She has written several books for children, including *Hornets*, *Medusa and Pegasus*, *From Wax to Crayons*, and *We Need Worms!*

About

Bookworms help independent readers gain reading confidence through high-frequency words, simple sentences, and strong picture/text support. Each book explores a concept that helps children relate what they read to the world they live in.